Original title:
The Rhythm of Relationships

Copyright © 2024 Swan Charm
All rights reserved.

Author: Lan Donne
ISBN HARDBACK: 978-9916-86-686-3
ISBN PAPERBACK: 978-9916-86-687-0
ISBN EBOOK: 978-9916-86-688-7

Steps in Sync

Together we walk, hand in hand,
Each step in rhythm, like grains of sand.
A dance of our hearts, a gentle embrace,
In the garden of trust, we find our place.

Through trials and storms, we stand so tall,
In the echoes of laughter, we hear the call.
With every heartbeat, our souls align,
In the tapestry of life, your hand in mine.

Paths may diverge, but we'll find a way,
Guided by love, we'll never stray.
In every shadow, a light will gleam,
With you by my side, we're a perfect team.

The world may turn, seasons may change,
Yet our connection will never feel strange.
Together we'll face whatever may come,
In the rhythm of life, we'll beat like a drum.

Lullabies of Loyalty

Whispers of promise in the night air,
Soft tunes of loyalty, beyond compare.
In the cradle of dreams, we gently sway,
With every breath, our love will stay.

Through the darkest hours, a beacon we shine,
In the heart of the storm, you're forever mine.
A symphony plays, wrapped in desire,
With each note we sing, our spirits aspire.

Beneath the stars, we find our song,
In harmony's embrace, we both belong.
With every lullaby, our souls entwine,
In the quiet of night, your heart is mine.

The waves may crash, the winds may roar,
But our bond is a river that flows to the shore.
As we dance through the night, let our dreams ignite,
In these lullabies of love, everything feels right.

Echoes in the Silence

In the depth of silence, whispers ignite,
Echoes of memories, shimmering light.
In the stillness, where shadows play,
We find the words we've left to say.

A gentle breeze carries tales of our past,
In the quiet, our bond holds steadfast.
With each breath drawn, a story unfolds,
In the heart of silence, our love it scolds.

The hush of the night sings of our fate,
In the echoes of moments, we contemplate.
With each lingering pause, our spirits entwine,
In the depths of the quiet, your heart beats with mine.

Through the void we traverse, hand in hand,
In the whispers of silence, we take a stand.
Beyond words spoken, a language divine,
In the echoes we find, love's sacred design.

Resonance of Understanding

In the dance of the stars, our truths align,
Beyond the words spoken, your heart knows mine.
In the depths of knowing, we gently sway,
With each shared glance, our souls convey.

In the silence between, our thoughts intertwine,
With every heartbeat, a rhythm divine.
The resonance grows in a space so rare,
In the warmth of connection, we breathe the air.

A tapestry woven with threads of grace,
In the fabric of time, we find our place.
In the storms we weather, side by side,
Through the trials of life, our hearts open wide.

With each step we take, we cherish the bond,
In the spaces of love, forever we're fond.
Through the ebb and flow, we rise and we fall,
In the resonance of understanding, we have it all.

Swaying Souls

In whispers soft as evening light,
Two hearts entwined take peaceful flight.
With every breath, they dance and sway,
In unity, they find their way.

Beneath the stars, a gentle glow,
Their silent truths begin to flow.
In tangled dreams, they find their grace,
A tender touch, a sweet embrace.

With every turn, the world stands still,
A symphony of heart and will.
Through storms that come and pass away,
Together, they will surely stay.

In rhythms soft, their spirits twine,
A bond unbroken, pure, divine.
As shadows fade and dawn breaks through,
Their love remains, forever true.

Symphonic Embrace

In melodies a heart can feel,
A symphony that makes it real.
Each note a promise wrapped in sound,
In music's arms, they both are found.

With every chord, they rise and fall,
An orchestra responding to their call.
In harmony, they share their fears,
And lift each other through the years.

The canvas painted with delight,
Their laughter ringing through the night.
As strings pull tighter, hearts align,
A dance composed, a love divine.

Each song a treasure, soft and bright,
Enveloping their world in light.
With every rhythm, hands entwined,
In symphonic love, they both are blind.

Tides of Trust

In waves that crash upon the shore,
Two souls found refuge, wanting more.
With every tide that pulls away,
They hold each other, come what may.

The ocean speaks in gentle tones,
With whispers soft as ocean's moans.
In depths of blue, their fears subside,
In currents strong, they will abide.

Each ebb and flow, a dance of fate,
They navigate, no room for hate.
With open hearts, they brave the storm,
In trust combines, a love so warm.

The horizon sings of what's to be,
In every wave, a memory.
With hands held tight, they ride the night,
Through tides of trust, to morning light.

Choreography of Hearts

In steps they take, the world's a stage,
A dance of love, a turning page.
With every glance, a movement flows,
In perfect sync, their passion glows.

With graceful twists and tender spins,
Two souls unite where joy begins.
In every leap, their spirits soar,
Their hearts choreographed for more.

The rhythm set, a beat so true,
In every step, they start anew.
As shadows blend, the light will chase,
The dance evolves, a sweet embrace.

From dusk to dawn, they glide and sway,
In choreography, love finds its way.
Together, lost in perfect art,
Forever joined, two beating hearts.

Patterns of Passion

In whispers soft, the flames arise,
Colors blend beneath the skies.
Fingers trace the tales we weave,
In every glance, we dare believe.

Hearts entwined in dance and song,
Echoes of where we belong.
Every smile, a silent vow,
In this moment, here and now.

Underneath the silver moon,
Time stands still, a perfect tune.
Each heartbeat echoes love's decree,
Together, we are wild and free.

Patterns drawn in seams of night,
Illuminate our shared delight.
With each breath, a promise made,
In this tapestry, we're laid.

As stars align and shadows fade,
Passion's light will never trade.
In the canvas of our souls,
Love's sweet patterns make us whole.

Echoes of Connection

In every laugh, a story waits,
Connections formed that fate narrates.
The gentle touch, a shared embrace,
In silent language, time finds grace.

Like rivers flowing, hearts collide,
In hidden spaces, love won't hide.
Each whisper shared, a bond anew,
Through echoes deep, I find you too.

The world may spin, yet we remain,
Tethered close through joy and pain.
In fleeting glances, sparks ignite,
Our connection shines, a beacon bright.

Through every struggle, every tear,
In the echoes, we find our cheer.
Resilient hearts, we rise and mend,
In every echo, love won't end.

So let the moments intertwine,
In threads of fate, our hearts align.
Embrace the journey, hand in hand,
In echoes deep, together stand.

Heartbeats in Harmony

Two souls dancing, side by side,
In perfect rhythm, hearts confide.
The music swells, the world fades out,
In harmony, we laugh and shout.

A gentle pulse, a soft refrain,
Together always, joy and pain.
In every heartbeat, life unfolds,
Love's sweet story, timeless, bold.

With every note, our spirits rise,
Underneath the vastest skies.
In vibrant hues, our passion glows,
A symphony the universe knows.

The tempo quickens, then it slows,
In this embrace, our journey flows.
United in the dance we share,
In heartbeats, we find the air.

In the twilight's soft embrace,
Our melodies intertwine with grace.
Bound by rhythms, souls converge,
In heartbeats, love will always surge.

Threads of Togetherness

Woven tightly, every thread,
In unity, we forge ahead.
Through storms that come and skies of blue,
Together, we'll make it, me and you.

In laughter shared and troubles faced,
Through every trial, our love is laced.
With each stitch, we build and grow,
In threads of warmth, our hearts aglow.

Like seasons change, so do we,
Yet hand in hand, we're wild and free.
In every twist, a story spun,
In togetherness, we become one.

In the quiet moments we create,
Through simple joys, we celebrate.
With every heartbeat, every sigh,
Our threads connect, they never die.

So let the world unwind and weave,
In every breath, we truly believe.
Bound by love, forever blessed,
In threads of togetherness, we rest.

Harmonizing Hearts

In the quiet of the night,
We share our dreams, take flight.
Soft whispers blend in tune,
Together, we sing to the moon.

Every note, a gentle kiss,
A melody wrapped in bliss.
Hearts aligned, like stars so bright,
Guided by love's pure light.

In the garden, flowers sway,
As we dance, come what may.
Echoes of laughter fill the air,
In this harmony, none can compare.

With each strum, our spirits soar,
A symphony we both adore.
United in rhythm, forever we'll be,
Two hearts bound in harmony.

As the world fades to gray,
Our song will always stay.
For in this bond, we'll never part,
Together, we harmonize our hearts.

Duets of Destiny

Across the stage, we meet,
Two voices, strong and sweet.
In the spotlight, hand in hand,
Together, we bravely stand.

Words weave a tale so grand,
In perfect sync, we understand.
Every challenge, side by side,
In this duet, we confide.

Moments shared, a magic spark,
Guiding us through the dark.
With each chorus, we ignite,
Our futures, shining bright.

In the dance of fate we move,
In every step, our hearts improve.
The world may sway, but we stay true,
A timeless bond between us two.

With every breath, we write our song,
In this duet, we both belong.
As the curtain slowly falls,
We'll cherish our destiny's calls.

Tones of Togetherness

In the chorus of our days,
We find warmth in gentle ways.
Notes of laughter fill the air,
In sweet moments, love's our care.

Side by side, we face the storm,
Creating joy, our hearts keep warm.
Each tone resonates, pure and near,
In the music, we persevere.

With every sigh, a note we play,
Through struggles faced, come what may.
In harmony, we stand as one,
Together, woven like the sun.

As raindrops fall, we find our beat,
In every challenge, love's our seat.
We dance through life with grace and cheer,
Our togetherness, crystal clear.

From dawn till dusk, let's write our song,
In the blend of us, we belong.
With tones that echo through the years,
In togetherness, we dry our tears.

Embracing the Unknown

In the shadows, courage grows,
Hand in hand, through highs and lows.
With trust, we take a step blind,
In the unknown, our hearts aligned.

The journey twists, yet we embrace,
Unraveling mysteries, we find our place.
With every heartbeat, secrets unfold,
In the thrill of fear, we're bold.

When the path is hard to see,
Together, we'll carve our destiny.
In the depths of uncertainty's space,
We find strength in love's embrace.

Moments fleeting, we hold tight,
Guided by passion, shining bright.
With wide-open hearts, we roam,
In the unknown, we build our home.

As the stars above give light,
We navigate through the night.
In the arms of chance, we'll grow,
Embracing the beauty of the unknown.

Heartbeat Echoes

In the stillness, whispers rise,
Soft reminders of our ties.
Every pulse, a gentle sway,
In your heart, I long to stay.

Moments shared in twilight glow,
Silent secrets, only we know.
Each heartbeat a soft embrace,
In this timeless, tender space.

Echoes linger, never fade,
In our world, love's serenade.
Through the chaos, find our way,
Together, come what may.

Life's rhythm, a sweet refrain,
Through the joy and through the pain.
With each step, we find our song,
In the dance where we belong.

Beneath the stars, we draw near,
In your gaze, I feel no fear.
Heartbeat echoes, true and free,
Here forever, you and me.

Dance of Togetherness

Underneath the moon's soft light,
We sway gently, hearts in flight.
With every turn, we find our grace,
In each step, we embrace space.

The world fades, only we exist,
In this moment, cannot resist.
Your hand in mine, a perfect fit,
Together, we shall never quit.

Melodies swirling in the air,
A rhythm born from love's sweet care.
In this dance, no room for doubt,
In our hearts, we sing it out.

Every twirl, a story told,
In your arms, I feel so bold.
A tapestry of light and sound,
In this dance, our love is found.

As the stars begin to gleam,
We step in time, a shared dream.
Dance of togetherness unfolds,
In each other, we find gold.

Tides of Connection

Waves crash softly on the shore,
With each pulse, we long for more.
Tides that rise and gently fall,
In your arms, I feel it all.

The ocean sings a timeless song,
A melody where we belong.
In the depths, our hearts entwine,
In the ebb, our souls align.

Moments like the rolling sea,
Changing but still constantly.
In the currents, we release,
Finding solace, finding peace.

With each tide, our bond will grow,
Like the moon, we ebb and flow.
In this dance of give and take,
A connection we cannot break.

Together, we will navigate,
Through life's journey, love's innate.
Tides of connection, pure and true,
In this wave, it's me and you.

Melodies of Us

In the quiet, you softly hum,
A tune that makes my heart succumb.
Every note a cherished sound,
In your love, I am spellbound.

With each chord, the world stands still,
As we chase a dream, a thrill.
In harmony, our voices blend,
Together, we shall never end.

Life's symphony, a grand array,
With you near, I find my way.
Notes of joy, whispers of pain,
In this melody, love will reign.

Guitar strings strum our delight,
Every song ignites the night.
Together, we'll create the score,
Melodies of us, forevermore.

In the rhythm, hearts collide,
Through every ebb, you're by my side.
With each tempo, our journey flows,
Forever singing, love bestows.

Harmonizing Troubles

In shadows deep, we search for light,
Holding hands through the night.
Whispers soft, hearts intertwine,
Together we rise, our spirits align.

When storms brew and tempests roar,
We find strength in each other's core.
Through trials faced, we sing our song,
In harmony, we learn to be strong.

Moments of doubt may come our way,
Yet in our bond, we find the sway.
With each note, we forge a path,
Turning sorrows into shared laughs.

So let the music guide our fate,
Weaving hope, never too late.
Through every struggle, we shall sway,
In our embrace, troubles fade away.

With voices raised, we pierce the night,
Finding peace in our shared flight.
Together we'll weather every storm,
For in our hearts, we are reborn.

Vows in the Wind

Beneath the stars, we make our pledge,
Promises whispered, love on the edge.
In the breeze, our secrets flow,
A bond so strong, it only grows.

In moments sweet, in silence pure,
Our hearts entwined, forever sure.
With every vow, we build our dreams,
In the night, we hear love's themes.

Through seasons change, we stand as one,
Facing the dawn, a new day begun.
In laughter shared and tears we dry,
With every heartbeat, we learn to fly.

In whispers soft, our spirits dance,
Each moment cherished, a second chance.
Together we soar, with love so wide,
In the wind, our dreams abide.

So take my hand, we'll run together,
Through storms and calm, in any weather.
Our vows like stars in the endless night,
Guiding us home, forever bright.

Dance of Understanding

In silence shared, we find our way,
A gentle nod, no words to say.
With every glance, a story told,
In rhythms soft, our hearts unfold.

Movements sway, as shadows play,
In this dance, we're led astray.
With open hearts, we seek to know,
In each step, love starts to grow.

Through differences, we learn and bend,
Finding strength in a common blend.
In every stumble, we rise again,
A harmony found in the sweetest refrain.

With hands held tight, we twirl and spin,
In this dance, we let hearts win.
Together we move, side by side,
In the dance of life, we take our stride.

So let the music play this night,
In the dance of understanding, we take flight.
With every beat, our souls ignite,
In this beautiful dance, everything feels right.

Flowing Through Moments

Like rivers winding, we flow along,
In every heartbeat, we find our song.
Through valleys low and mountains high,
In each moment, we learn to fly.

With laughter bright and shadows cast,
We cherish memories, hold them fast.
In fleeting time, we find our grace,
In every smile, a warm embrace.

As seasons change and days unfold,
We gather stories, both new and old.
In the flow, we learn to stay,
Finding joy in the everyday.

Letting go, we drift like leaves,
In nature's rhythm, our spirit weaves.
From dawn to dusk, we'll dance and play,
Learning to live in each moment's sway.

So take my hand, let's flow as one,
In this journey, our hearts are spun.
Through every moment, let's embrace,
As we flow through life, finding our place.

Echoing Emotions

Whispers dance in twilight light,
Shadows play, then take their flight.
Heartbeats echo deep within,
Memories fade, yet still they spin.

Silent tears on weathered cheeks,
Words unsaid, the heart still speaks.
Every smile a fleeting spark,
Hope ignites within the dark.

Branches sway like gentle sighs,
As the night begins to rise.
Emotions flow like tides at sea,
Yearning souls for harmony.

In the stillness, secrets swell,
Like the stories all could tell.
Echoes of a time now past,
In our hearts, they forever last.

Time will blend both pain and bliss,
In each moment, find a kiss.
Embrace the whispers of the night,
In the shadows, find your light.

Staccato Steps

Tap, tap, the rhythm starts,
A journey forged from beating hearts.
Each step sharp, precise, and clear,
Marking paths for all to hear.

Bouncing lightly on the ground,
Magic woven all around.
Life's a dance of quick delight,
Movement flows like stars at night.

Every pause, a silent breath,
In the dance, we flirt with death.
Yet, in the beats, we find our way,
Guided by the words we say.

Step to the echoing beat,
Feel the pulse beneath your feet.
Staccato dreams in vibrant hues,
Painting life with every muse.

Together, we define the days,
In our steps, unique displays.
Each moment cherished, none we rue,
In staccato, we find what's true.

Chords of Connection

Strummed on strings, a melody,
Bound by love eternally.
Harmony woven through our veins,
In every joy and all our pains.

Notes collide and gently soar,
Each moment felt, we crave for more.
Fingers dance across the frets,
In shared echoes, no regrets.

Tuning hearts to perfect grace,
In this song, we've found our place.
Chords of laughter, chords of tears,
Together, we have faced our fears.

With every strum, our spirits rise,
In this music, no disguise.
Threads of sound, a vibrant thread,
Binding us as we are led.

In the silence, love resounds,
In every heart, a song abounds.
Through each note, we come alive,
In our connection, we will thrive.

Uniting Under the Stars

Beneath the vast and twinkling light,
We gather close, hearts burning bright.
Constellations whisper dreams anew,
In the night, I find you true.

Hands entwined, as shadows fade,
In the moment, promises made.
Voices mingling in the breeze,
Stories shared bring us to our knees.

Every star a guiding ray,
Leading us through night to day.
In this cosmic dance we find,
A unity that's intertwined.

Time stands still, the world withdraws,
In this embrace, eternal cause.
Wonder lingers in the air,
Lifting hopes beyond compare.

Together we light the darkened skies,
As constellations hear our sighs.
In every heartbeat, in every glance,
Uniting under stars, we dance.

Harmonies in Motion

In a world where rhythms play,
Life dances softly, night and day.
Melodies rise like the morning sun,
Each note a journey, a race begun.

Wind whispers tales of distant dreams,
Laughter echoes in sunlight beams.
Hearts entwined in sweet refrain,
Together we weave joy and pain.

Footsteps linger on the ground,
With each beat, new hopes are found.
The pulse of life, a timeless song,
In every heart, we all belong.

Stars align in cosmic grace,
Every moment, a sacred space.
As we twirl through shadows cast,
Futures bright, releasing the past.

Harmonies rise and gently fade,
In this dance, our fears unmade.
Voices blend in vibrant hues,
In motion, love is our muse.

A Symphony of Souls

Beneath the stars, our spirits soar,
In every heart, there's an open door.
We share a rhythm, a sacred call,
In this symphony, we rise and fall.

Notes intertwine like vines that grow,
In each embrace, our feelings flow.
Together we craft a timeless tale,
Where love prevails, and dreams set sail.

Softest whispers touch the night,
With each heartbeat, we feel the light.
Echoes of laughter mingle with tears,
Binding us closer through all the years.

A melody born from hope and grace,
In every challenge, we find our place.
The music swells, a poignant prize,
In this grand ballet, we realize.

As shadows dance, and twilight gleams,
In the harmony of our shared dreams.
A symphony that soars above,
We are the music, we are the love.

Beats Beneath the Surface

Beneath the waves, a rhythm beats,
In silence, our heart's song repeats.
Echoes of dreams lie deep below,
Where hopes and fears collectively flow.

A pulse of life in shadows cast,
In the depths, we are free at last.
Hidden currents, stories untold,
In every moment, rich and bold.

Quiet whispers in the dark,
Awakened souls, we leave our mark.
The dance of water, light and air,
In every breath, an adventure rare.

Beneath the calm, the storms may rage,
Yet we find peace in the sacred page.
Through valleys deep and mountains high,
We seek the truth that lies nearby.

A symphony of beats we hear,
In the whispers of those we hold dear.
We dive deep, where the light is sparse,
In the depths, we find our part.

Choreography of Emotions

In the dance of shadows and light,
We move to the rhythm of day and night.
Every step a story, every spin a charm,
In this choreography, we feel warm.

Hearts with grace, we intertwine,
In every glance, a spark divine.
The cadence of laughter, the sigh of dreams,
Each moment flows with gentle streams.

With whispers soft, we navigate,
Through twists and turns, we celebrate.
In the silence, our souls will speak,
In movements bold, we find the peak.

A tapestry woven with threads of fate,
Every heartbeat, a chance to create.
In the ebb and flow, we find our role,
In this grand dance, we become whole.

Our emotions rise, a vivid sea,
In the rhythm of love, we are free.
Choreography of the heart's pure song,
Together we dance, where we all belong.

The Pulse of Us

In shadows cast by fading light,
Two hearts beat softly, synchronized.
An echo whispers through the night,
A rhythm born where love resides.

United dreams in every glance,
A dance of souls, entwined in fate.
With every heartbeat, we advance,
The pulse of us, a bond innate.

Through storms that rage and winds that wail,
We'll stand as one, our spirits strong.
The melody of love won't fail,
In harmony, we both belong.

Each moment shared, a thread, a spark,
A tapestry of joy, unspooled.
In light and dark, within the arc,
The pulse of us is love, renewed.

As time flows on like rivers wide,
We'll write our tale, an endless song.
In every heartbeat, side by side,
The pulse of us will guide us long.

Resonant Emotions

In silence deep, where feelings grow,
Resonance lingers, softly felt.
Each wave a story, ebb and flow,
Emotions bloom, like flowers knelt.

Beyond the words that dance in air,
A language spoken by the soul.
In every sigh, a secret share,
Resonant emotions, making whole.

With laughter bright, through tears we trod,
A symphony of highs and lows.
The fragile thread that binds and nods,
In resonance, our love still glows.

Through trials faced and dreams pursued,
Our hearts compose a sacred song.
In every note, a hope imbued,
Resonant emotions, where we belong.

As time slips by like whispered breeze,
We'll hold these feelings, vast and wide.
In harmony, we find our ease,
Resonant emotions will abide.

Chasing Echoes

In moonlit dreams, we drift away,
Chasing echoes, both soft and sweet.
Each whispered word, a soft ballet,
A fleeting dance where hearts will meet.

Through valleys deep and mountains high,
We seek the sounds that linger near.
In twilight's glow, we reach for sky,
Chasing echoes, lost in cheer.

With every step, a story made,
In echoes born from love's embrace.
Through winds of change, our voices played,
The past resounds in time and space.

Across the waves, we hear the calls,
Old memories wrapped in soft refrain.
In every shadow, laughter falls,
Chasing echoes, joy and pain.

As night unfolds its velvet cloak,
We'll roam the paths where dreams reside.
In every echo, love awoke,
Chasing echoes, hearts as guide.

Balancing Beats

In a world of chaos, we find grace,
Balancing beats, a dance divine.
With every step, we find our place,
In rhythm, hearts in perfect line.

Guided by stars, we flow and sway,
With gentle grace, the music plays.
In harmony's arms, we'll drift away,
Balancing beats through night and days.

Each pulse a story, each turn a chance,
We weave our dreams on life's grand stage.
In every heartbeat, love's sweet dance,
Balancing beats, a timeless page.

Through moments fleeting, we embrace,
The tempo shifts, yet still we hold.
In every laugh, in every trace,
Balancing beats, a love of gold.

With every breath, we find our tone,
In sync, our spirits soar and rise.
Together conquering the unknown,
Balancing beats, we touch the skies.

Flourish of Synergy

In gardens where hopes entwine,
Soft whispers bloom, intertwine.
Hands join in a vibrant dance,
Nature thrives in a shared stance.

Beneath the sun's warm embrace,
Seeds of trust find their place.
Together we grow, strong and free,
In the heart of unity's spree.

Winds of change gently blow,
As rivers of purpose flow.
Each voice adds to the refrain,
A harmony boundless, no chain.

Roots delve deep in the earth,
Celebrating shared worth.
In every petal, a dream,
Together we thrive, a team.

Through storms and sunny days,
We'll navigate countless ways.
With laughter and love as our guide,
In this journey, we abide.

Crescendo of Care

In a world where hopes collide,
Tender hearts swell with pride.
Each act of kindness, a note,
Composing love's gentle quote.

A melody of embrace,
Leaves a sweet and lasting trace.
Together, we rise, we soar,
As the chorus calls for more.

Every glance, a soft reply,
Beneath the vast, open sky.
With compassion as our score,
We find strength to explore.

Healing hands and listening ears,
Calming even our deepest fears.
In the symphony of the heart,
Each note plays an essential part.

The crescendo lifts us high,
Like birds dancing through the sky.
In unity, we hold the light,
Creating beauty, pure and bright.

The Dance of Devotion

In twilight's hush, we sway,
Two souls lost in the play.
With every step, a tale told,
In warmth that drives out the cold.

Our shadows merge on the floor,
A rhythm we can't ignore.
With eyes that gleam and minds in sync,
In this moment, we don't think.

Spinning memories in the air,
With every twirl, a whispered prayer.
In the dance of give and take,
United, our hearts awake.

As the stars begin to shine,
We find each heartbeat aligns.
In the stillness, a vow we make,
Together, for love's sweet sake.

In every dip, in every spin,
Our souls weave together, akin.
In the dance, forever bound,
In devotion, love is found.

Mutual Meters

In sync we breathe, two lives as one,
A rhythm of pulses, a song begun.
Each heartbeat echoes the other's care,
In moments shared, our spirits bare.

With each step taken, our paths align,
A dance of dreams, both yours and mine.
Through laughter and trials, we navigate,
The meters of love we create.

In tender whispers that softly flow,
Like rivers that wind, our feelings grow.
In each touch, a promise sincere,
Together we'll conquer every fear.

As we chart the course of our days,
Our hearts compose intricate arrays.
Through harmony, we find our place,
In the cadence of love's embrace.

And when the world seems out of tune,
We find our rhythm beneath the moon.
In mutual meters, we shall thrive,
A symphony of love, alive.

Navigating the Nuances

In shadows and light, we find our way,
Through whispers of doubt, we choose to stay.
Each turn a lesson, each glance a guide,
In the dance of the heart, we won't divide.

With colors that blend, we paint our scene,
Finding our rhythm, both smooth and keen.
The map is unwritten, the journey is ours,
Navigating life beneath the stars.

Through tempest and calm, we chart the course,
With every heartbeat, we feel the force.
Together we venture, hand in hand tight,
In the tapestry woven from day to night.

In moments of silence, or laughter's embrace,
We uncover the nuances of time and space.
Each tear and each smile forms the whole,
Navigating the depths, enriching the soul.

Love's Collective Chorus

In symphonies sweet, our hearts align,
Every note a promise, a love divine.
Together we sing, a harmonious blend,
In this collective chorus, our voices ascend.

Through highs and lows, our spirits will soar,
Each melody crafted, forevermore.
A rhythm of trust, each beat we share,
Building a legacy, beyond compare.

With echoes of laughter, our anthem grows,
In the stillness of night, sweet repose flows.
Love is the song that we both compose,
In this timeless dance, endlessly flows.

In each heartbeat's echo, we find our theme,
A love that unites, more than it seems.
Together we harmonize, bright and clear,
In love's collective chorus, we persevere.

Syncopation of Sentiments

In the heartbeat of moments, we find our sway,
In the rhythm of love, we dance and play.
With each breath we take, feel the change,
Syncopation of sentiments, beautifully strange.

Emotions collide like waves on the shore,
In the space between silence, we crave for more.
A spark in the night, a flicker of hope,
Together we learn, together we cope.

With laughter like music, we twirl and spin,
Through the light and the dark, our treasures within.
A tapestry woven with threads of our dreams,
In syncopation of love, nothing's as it seems.

We embrace the chaos, the highs and the lows,
In the dance of our hearts, the passion still flows.
With every misstep, we find our way back,
In rhythm and rhyme, love's sacred track.

Tapestry of Together

Every thread a story, intricately spun,
In the tapestry of together, we are one.
Crafting our fate with each moment shared,
Woven in kindness, deeply cared.

Through laughter and trials, our fabric is strong,
In colors of courage, we both belong.
Each stitch a memory, tender and bright,
In the tapestry of life, we face the light.

With visions entwined, our dreams interlace,
In the warmth of your presence, I find my place.
A blend of our hearts, forever known,
In this work of art, love has grown.

As seasons may change, our bond remains true,
In the tapestry of together, it's me and you.
Each moment a treasure, each day a delight,
In the fabric of time, we shine so bright.

Waltz of Vulnerability

In shadows where we dare to fall,
Our hearts exposed, we hear the call.
With trembling steps, we dance so near,
In this soft sway, we shed our fear.

The rhythm guides our whispered sighs,
Each moment shared, a sweet surprise.
As secrets bloom like starry skies,
We find our truth in gentle lies.

With every twirl, the scars reveal,
The tender touch that wounds can heal.
In open arms, we boldly sway,
In vulnerability, we play.

The music swells as spirits rise,
Two souls entwined in dark and light.
In this embrace, we find the grace,
To waltz together through the night.

As dawn approaches, shadows fade,
The courage found, the choices made.
In love's own dance, we find our way,
A waltz of hearts that choose to stay.

Intertwined Journeys

Two paths converge upon the ground,
In every step, a love profound.
Through winding trails and skies so blue,
We share the weight of dreams anew.

Each journey tells a tale of old,
With stories shared, our hearts unfold.
In laughter bright, and tears that flow,
Together, side by side, we grow.

With every turn, we blaze the way,
In challenges, we choose to stay.
For beauty lies in what we share,
In every moment, in every care.

The compass guides, but hearts will steer,
Through storms and calm, we persevere.
As chapters turn, our bond will shine,
In every step, your hand in mine.

In twilight's glow, our paths ignite,
With dreams as vast as the night.
Through intertwined journeys that we roam,
We build together, a lasting home.

Ballad of Belonging

In places where our laughter rings,
In every heart, a song that sings.
With open arms, we greet the dawn,
In unity, we all belong.

Through trials faced, and joys we find,
In shared embraces, hearts aligned.
The tapestry of lives we weave,
In threads of hope, we can believe.

Across the miles, our spirits soar,
For love unites, and opens doors.
In every hug, in every smile,
We banish fears, if just awhile.

The streets we walk, the dreams we chase,
In every moment, a sacred space.
In simple truths that weave our song,
We find our place, we all belong.

So let us linger, hold the light,
In the warmth of friendship's sight.
In every heartbeat that we share,
We craft a world beyond compare.

Sonnet of Shared Dreams

In twilight's glow where whispers meet,
We weave the threads of dreams so sweet.
Through starlit skies, our hopes take flight,
In shared visions, we find our light.

Each promise made beneath the stars,
Our hearts entwined through endless bars.
With every dream, we chase the dawn,
Together strong, we carry on.

With every tear and laughter's gleam,
We paint a world born from our dream.
In every challenge, we grow bold,
Our story's worth more than gold.

So hand in hand, we'll face the stream,
Forever bound in this grand scheme.
In love and trust, we'll always find,
The magic held in hearts aligned.

Tangles and Ties

In the garden of whispers, we meet,
Threads of laughter, soft and sweet.
With every turn, a knot appears,
Binding moments, shaping our fears.

Fingers entwined, we navigate,
The paths of life, the hands of fate.
Through tangled woods, we learn to trust,
In bonds unbroken, a must.

Our hearts like vines, they twist and twine,
Creating a bond that feels divine.
In storms we weather, in calm we stay,
Tangled together, come what may.

Every smile, a gentle cue,
Each glance shared, a love that's true.
In this maze, we find our way,
With ties that hold, come what may.

Together we dance, a wild ballet,
In this symphony, let's not stray.
For in the chaos, there lies the key,
Tangles and ties, just you and me.

Harmonies in the Moonlight

Under the glow of silver rays,
We weave our dreams in gentle ways.
The night sings softly, a timeless tune,
In perfect rhythm, with the moon.

Each note we share, a tender grace,
In shadows cast, we find our place.
Where silence speaks, and hearts align,
Their pulse the same, a love divine.

Beneath the stars, our secrets rise,
In whispered tales, we touch the skies.
With every laugh, and whispered sigh,
Harmony blooms as time slips by.

The evening breeze, a gentle guide,
Together we sail, in joy we ride.
With melodies sweet, our spirits soar,
In moonlight's embrace, we want nothing more.

So let us dance, in twilight's charm,
With every heartbeat, there lies no harm.
In this moment, forever stay,
Harmonies hum, as night turns to day.

Vibrations of Vulnerability

In a world of armor, I stand bare,
Holding my fears, exposed to air.
Each trembling step, a shaky dance,
In the light of truth, I take my chance.

Waves of honesty crash and roll,
With every heartbeat, I reveal my soul.
In this softness, a strength I find,
A bond that forms when hearts unwind.

The scars we carry tell our tale,
In the winds of life, we set our sail.
Through tears that fall like gentle rain,
We learn to love, embrace the pain.

Sharing pieces, bit by bit,
In these moments, we softly sit.
With every layer shed, we grow,
Vibrations merge, a tender flow.

For in the rawness, beauty stands,
With open hearts, we join our hands.
In vulnerability's gentle light,
We find our way, together, right.

Sonata of Friendship

In laughter's rhythm, we share our days,
Through highs and lows, in countless ways.
A melody woven, with care and grace,
In this grand sonata, we find our place.

With every note, a story told,
In the tapestry of life, rich and bold.
We harmonize through laughter and tears,
In the symphony crafted by years.

Together we rise, like songs in the sun,
In the heart's orchestra, we are one.
A gentle chorus that never fades,
In friendship's embrace, love cascades.

With open hearts, we play each part,
In this timeless piece, we pour our heart.
Through every measure, our spirits sing,
In the sonata of life, friendship's the king.

Let's dance through moments, soft and loud,
In cherished bonds, forever proud.
With every crescendo, our spirits lift,
This sonata of friendship, our greatest gift.

Euphony of Empathy

In every heart a rhythm flows,
A gentle touch where kindness grows.
We stand together, hand in hand,
Creating bonds across the land.

Through tales of joy and tales of pain,
We find the strength to break each chain.
With every story, we inspire,
A symphony of hearts on fire.

Let voices rise, let shadows wane,
In unity, we break the chain.
With open hearts, we learn to feel,
In euphony, our souls we heal.

Symphonic Secrets

Whispers of truth in melodies,
Secrets tied in harmonies.
Each note a key, each pause a sign,
Unlocking worlds, both yours and mine.

In shadows cast by fading light,
The music swells, dispelling night.
Together we will seek the rare,
Symphonic secrets in the air.

With every chord, the heart will soar,
In symphonic dreams, we will explore.
Together bound by love and sound,
In every heartbeat, peace is found.

Vibrations of Values

Echoes of trust in every breath,
Values that thrive beyond all death.
In every word, intent is clear,
A ripple born from love and fear.

Resilience shines in darkest days,
Guiding lights in life's tough maze.
Together standing, firm but kind,
In vibrations, our paths aligned.

With courage stitched in every seam,
We weave a fabric of our dream.
Through love, respect, and dignity,
We shape a world of harmony.

Journey as One

Footsteps echo on the path we tread,
A journey shared, where dreams are led.
In unity, we rise and fall,
Together we can conquer all.

With every step, a brand new start,
With open minds and open hearts.
The road may twist, but we stay true,
Our bonds, they strengthen as we move.

In every corner of this place,
We find our strength in each embrace.
As one we journey, hand in hand,
Together we create a land.

Melting into Mirth

In laughter's warm embrace, we find,
A joy so pure, it frees the mind.
With every smile, our spirits lift,
Moments shared, the greatest gift.

The sun spills gold on laughter's face,
In every heart, a sacred space.
We dance beneath the sky so bright,
Melting into mirth, pure delight.

With giggles soft, like whispered dreams,
We flow together, or so it seems.
In every chuckle, a bond we weave,
In joy and play, we truly believe.

Through seasons of both joy and pain,
We'll cherish laughter, like sweet rain.
Each note of mirth, a song we sing,
Together in joy, it's everything.

So let us laugh, let spirits soar,
In this embrace, we want for more.
Melting into mirth, hearts aligned,
In every moment, love we find.

Rhythmic Bonds

In the dance of life, we find our beat,
A heart that echoes in every street.
With every step, our spirits blend,
Through rhythmic bonds, we transcend.

The world moves close, each hand in hand,
Together we rise, together we stand.
Each heartbeat mirrors the ties we forge,
In the pulse of time, our dreams enlarge.

Songs of unity fill the air,
In every note, a world we share.
As hearts align, the music flows,
With rhythmic bonds, our patience grows.

In laughter's cadence, in sorrow's plea,
We'll find our path, you and me.
Each moment danced, a love profound,
In this embrace, we're forever bound.

So let the rhythm guide our way,
With every beat, we seize the day.
In sync with life, our spirits sing,
Through rhythmic bonds, our hearts take wing.

Tonality of Together

In harmony we find our song,
A symphony where we belong.
Each note a dream, a hope expressed,
In the tonality of together, we're blessed.

The world sings soft, a gentle tune,
Underneath the sun and moon.
With voices raised and hearts in sync,
Together, we sip from love's sweet drink.

In melodies entwined, we grow,
With every rhythm, love set aglow.
In trials faced, we find our way,
The tonality of together will stay.

Through highs and lows, we weave the sound,
In this embrace, we're always found.
Each chord a promise, forever true,
In the tonality, it's me and you.

So let our hearts continue to rhyme,
In every season, across all time.
Together we rise, together we soar,
In the tonality of love, evermore.

Steps in Sync

With each step, we find our place,
In this dance of life, a shared space.
With rhythm guiding our gentle sway,
Steps in sync, come what may.

Each twirl reveals a trust profound,
In every spin, we're love unbound.
With laughter echoing in the air,
Steps in sync, a bond so rare.

Through trials faced, our feet won't part,
In unison, we dance from the heart.
With every stride, we journey on,
Steps in sync till the break of dawn.

Together we tread on paths unknown,
In every step, our strength has grown.
With courage shared, we face life's brink,
In every heartbeat, our hearts think.

So take my hand, let's face the day,
With steps in sync, we'll find our way.
In the dance of life, forever true,
Steps in sync, just me and you.

Dialogues in Motion

Words collide like waves,
In the storm of chance.
Echoes of laughter ring,
As thoughts take their dance.

Steps trace the heartbeat,
In shadows so light.
Conversations drift softly,
Through day into night.

Paths crisscross gently,
In the silent air.
Every glance a story,
A moment to share.

With hopes intertwined,
Together we flow.
In the canvas of dreams,
Our colors will glow.

Stories unfurling wide,
In the flicker of time.
A journey in whispers,
Where thoughts brightly climb.

Lullabies of Loyalty

In quiet of night,
A promise takes flight.
Soft whispers surround,
In love's gentle light.

A bond without chains,
Through mischief and bliss.
Hearts beat in rhythm,
In unwavering kiss.

Stars twinkle above,
As secrets unfold.
In trust we find peace,
A warmth to behold.

Through trials and tears,
Together we stand.
With hands intertwined,
In this loyal land.

In moments of doubt,
A beacon shines bright.
Like lullabies sung,
Through the darkest night.

Balancing on a Tightrope

Life poised on a thread,
Between joy and pain.
Each step a decision,
A delicate gain.

Winds whisper and blow,
Testing the stance.
Courage is needed,
For every small chance.

Wobbling forward,
With dreams in the air.
Focus on the end,
With courage to spare.

The thrill of the height,
Ignites every fear.
But laughter erupts,
As the end draws near.

With arms open wide,
To embrace the fall,
Balancing on life's rope,
To rise through it all.

Notes of Nostalgia

In corners of memory,
Echoes softly play.
Faded photographs,
Of a long-lost day.

Each note a reminder,
Of laughter and tears.
Melodies linger sweet,
Through the passing years.

The scent of the seasons,
In stories retold.
Warm hugs of a friend,
In the heart's hold.

Time stitches together,
The fabric of life.
Threads woven with care,
Through joy and strife.

In the glow of twilight,
We cherish the past.
With notes of nostalgia,
Our moments will last.

Swirls of Surrender

In twilight's glow, we find our peace,
Whispers of the wind, a soft release.
Letting go of all our fears,
In the dance of time, our hearts adhere.

Moonlit paths where shadows play,
Fading echoes, dreams on display.
Surrendering to the night sky's call,
Finding strength within the fall.

Embracing what the stars impart,
Each beat a tale, a work of art.
Swirling thoughts in a cosmic flow,
With every breath, we learn to grow.

Tides of change in gentle hands,
Waves of grace across the lands.
In the quiet, wisdom's found,
In swirls of surrender, lost and bound.

With every dawn, a brand new start,
In the silence, we guard the heart.
Embracing beauty in the unknown,
In surrender, we find our home.

Dance of Distances

Across the miles, our spirits flow,
In the distance, love's seeds we sow.
Every heartbeat, a step we take,
In the dance of distances, bonds we make.

Fleeting gazes, a touch of grace,
Through the spaces, we find our place.
Echoing laughter in the air,
A waltz of memories, we both share.

Time may stretch, but hearts remain,
In the rhythm of longing, joy, and pain.
Countless stars between us glow,
In this dance, our spirits grow.

Moments caught in a gentle breeze,
Carried softly like rustling leaves.
Through the silence, we understand,
The dance of distances, hand in hand.

Though apart, our souls entwined,
In every step, our hearts aligned.
Stars may wander, but love persists,
In this dance, we coexist.

Murmurs of Memory

Whispers from the past, so sweet,
In the depths of time, we meet.
Tales of laughter, echoes of tears,
Murmurs of memory through the years.

Faded photos in soft light,
Rekindling dreams that take to flight.
Each moment held within the heart,
In these whispers, we play our part.

Ghostly shadows in the room,
Memories blossom, tinged with bloom.
Tender stories that intertwine,
In the silence, our souls align.

Through the corridors of olden days,
Nostalgic moments in subtle ways.
Every whisper a gentle grace,
Murmurs of memory we embrace.

In the tapestry of years gone by,
A gentle sigh, a fleeting high.
Held in time, forever yours,
Murmurs of memory, love endures.

Strains of Support

In the shadows, we stand so tall,
With open hearts, we catch the fall.
A gentle hand, a guiding light,
Strains of support through day and night.

Every burden shared, a lift,
In solidarity, love's great gift.
Voices rise like songs in the air,
In the strength of many, we find care.

Through valleys deep, or mountains high,
We walk together, you and I.
In quiet moments, strength is found,
Strains of support, our hearts unbound.

Together we rise, through stormy weather,
In unity, we're light as a feather.
With every step, we pave the way,
In strains of support, we'll never sway.

Hand in hand, we face the dawn,
In every struggle, love goes on.
Embracing strength, our spirits soar,
In strains of support, we are more.

Dancing to Love's Melody

In twilight's embrace, we spin and sway,
With every twirl, worries drift away.
A rhythm found in heartbeats aligned,
Together we dance, our souls intertwined.

The stars above watch with shining eyes,
Guiding our steps as the night softly sighs.
With laughter echoing in the still air,
Our love's sweet melody, beyond compare.

The moon casts shadows where dreams take flight,
In the warmth of your arms, everything feels right.
Each movement a promise, a vow we share,
In this dance of love, every moment we care.

The music plays on, a timeless refrain,
With every step forward, we break every chain.
Together as one, in this vibrant display,
Dancing to love's song, we'll never stray.

So hold me close as the night stretches long,
In the dance of our hearts, we always belong.
With passion ignited, our spirits set free,
We're dancing to love's sweet melody.

Whispers of Affection

In quiet corners, soft voices rise,
Whispers of love beneath starry skies.
Each word a caress, a promise so dear,
In the hush of the night, our hearts draw near.

Moments of silence wrapped in a sigh,
Glimmers of warmth like the fireflies.
We speak in glances, in touches so light,
Every whisper a flame, igniting the night.

Through gentle breezes, our secrets are shared,
In the tapestry of dreams, we're beautifully paired.
These whispers of affection, soft as a breeze,
Bring comfort and joy, like honeyed bees.

With every heartbeat, our bond grows strong,
In the chorus of love, where we both belong.
Let the world fade away, it's just you and me,
Whispers of affection, our sweet symphony.

So lean in closer, let our souls entwine,
In this quiet space, your heart mirrors mine.
Together we weave these whispers anew,
A tapestry woven from me and from you.

Cadence of Companionship

In every journey, side by side we roam,
With laughter and love, we make our home.
The cadence of life in sync as we tread,
Two hearts beating softly, where others have fled.

With every stumble, you're there to catch,
In the rhythm of trust, there's nothing to match.
Through trials we dance, through joy we glide,
In the cadence of companionship, there's nothing to hide.

Together we share both the sun and the rain,
Each moment a treasure, each loss a gain.
With stories entwined, our narratives blend,
In this dance of support, we never pretend.

So here's to the moments, each whispered sigh,
In the warmth of your smile, I feel I can fly.
The cadence we follow, unique and divine,
In the heart of my being, I know you are mine.

As seasons will change, our love will remain,
In the rhythm of life, through joy and through pain.
With every heartbeat, my friend, you will see,
Our cadence of companionship is pure harmony.

Beats of Bonding

In the heart of the moment, we find our beat,
With every shared glance, our lives feel complete.
Each laughter echoes like a bubble released,
In the dance of the day, we're joyful at least.

From coffee-stained mornings to starlit nights,
We create our own rhythm, where everything's right.
In the beats of bonding, a story unfolds,
Whispered adventures more precious than gold.

Through every heartbeat, our connection grows,
In the garden of life, love wildly flows.
The music of friendship resounds in the air,
Encapsulating moments, showing we care.

With hands intertwined, we face what may come,
In the harmony of life, we'll never succumb.
For in every heartbeat, you're part of my song,
These beats of bonding, where we both belong.

So here is to laughter, to love, and to trust,
In the symphony of life, it's you I must.
As the rhythm continues, we stand hand in hand,
In the beats of bonding, together we'll stand.

Interlude of Laughter

In the garden of joy, we play,
Echoes of giggles light the day.
Bubbles of mirth dance on air,
Worries dissolve, nothing to bear.

Sunshine spills on cheerful faces,
Time slows down in happy places.
Every chuckle, a gentle spark,
Filling the world, chasing the dark.

Moments shared in gleeful delight,
Laughter blooms, vibrant and bright.
Whispers of joy weave in the breeze,
Crafting memories, hearts at ease.

Joyous notes of life collide,
In the rhythm, we take pride.
Celebrate no matter how small,
Interlude of laughter, embracing all.

With every chuckle, we let go,
Sharing warmth in laughter's glow.
In this dance, we find our song,
Together in laughter, we all belong.

Flows of Forgiveness

In the river where silence flows,
Gentle currents mend all woes.
Hearts entwined in soft release,
Inviting peace, granting sweet cease.

Whispers of love break the chain,
Old grievances washed away, no pain.
Each ripple tells a story untold,
Bridges built, no longer cold.

Embracing the warmth of the sun,
Healing begins when we've begun.
With every tide, we learn to bend,
Finding strength to rest and mend.

Like the moon guiding the night,
Forgiveness illuminates our plight.
In clarity, we find our grace,
Flows of forgiveness, a warm embrace.

Letting go, we rise anew,
With every breath, we feel the blue.
Flows of forgiveness, a sacred art,
Uniting the world, healing the heart.

Chorus of Change

The winds carry whispers of fate,
Change unfolds, never too late.
In every heartbeat, a new refrain,
Life's symphony, embracing the rain.

Mountains shift beneath our feet,
Finding courage in each heartbeat.
As seasons turn, we learn to grow,
Chorus of change, letting life flow.

Every dawn brings a fresh start,
Transforming shadows within the heart.
With open minds, we pave the way,
Chasing dreams and brightening day.

Nature sings in vibrant hues,
Coloring skies with greens and blues.
In unison, we rise, we soar,
Chorus of change, forevermore.

Through trials faced, we stand tall,
Change weaves strength into our call.
Together we sing, a resonant sound,
Embracing the journey, love unbound.

Tones of Trust

In the silence, a bond is found,
Tones of trust in whispers surround.
Glimmers of truth in every glance,
Building bridges, a sacred dance.

Through laughter shared and tears that flow,
Trust deepens, like seeds we sow.
In open hearts, vulnerability lies,
Painting our world with honest skies.

Hands reaching out, a gentle touch,
In the symphony, we find so much.
Every word, a note so clear,
Tones of trust, we hold dear.

With each promise made and kept,
In shared stories, connection leapt.
Together we weather the storm's sway,
Tones of trust guide every day.

Let us nurture this sacred space,
With kindness and love, we embrace.
In every heartbeat, we find the way,
Tones of trust, forever we stay.

Verses of Vows

In quiet whispers, we made our pact,
A bond unbroken, a shared abstract.
With every heartbeat, our words align,
In sacred silence, your hand in mine.

Through trials faced and joys embraced,
We weave our dreams, in love encased.
For every promise, a treasure found,
In life's great dance, forever bound.

With honest hearts, we stand as one,
In laughter's light and shadows spun.
Together we bloom, in sunlight's glow,
As seasons shift, our love will grow.

Each vow a thread, a tapestry bright,
Reflecting warmth in the dark of night.
With hope as our guide, we'll journey wide,
No fear in our hearts, with love as our pride.

In every moment, a chance to say,
We choose each other, come what may.
And in the twilight, when dreams arise,
We'll find our strength in each other's eyes.

Cadences of Closeness

In gentle rhythm, our hearts entwined,
With every glance, a spark aligned.
The softest whispers caress the night,
In your embrace, everything feels right.

Through valleys low and mountains high,
Together we laugh, together we sigh.
In shared secrets, our souls connect,
In every heartbeat, we both reflect.

With every step, we write our song,
A melody sweet, where we belong.
In silences shared, our spirits soar,
With you beside me, I need nothing more.

The cadence of closeness, a dance divine,
Each moment cherished, your hand in mine.
Like stars above, we shine so bright,
In this beautiful symphony of light.

As shadows fade, and dawn draws near,
In your laughter, I find my cheer.
With every heartbeat, a bond divine,
In this rhythm of love, forever we shine.

Polyphony of Promises

In harmony's embrace, our voices blend,
A promise made, a love to tend.
With every note, our spirits rise,
In this symphony, affection flies.

Each vow a verse, in time's sweet song,
Through every challenge, we stand strong.
In the echo of dreams, we find our way,
In the light of dawn, we greet the day.

With laughter's tune and hope's refrain,
We dance through life, through joy and pain.
In whispered prayers and glowing light,
Our hearts entwined, we take flight.

A polyphony rich, each promise clear,
In the stillness, I'll always hear.
Together we rise, together we fall,
In this grand concert, we give our all.

As music flows, so does our fate,
In every heartbeat, love resonates.
In the tapestry woven, our lives will sing,
In the chorus of love, forever spring.

Intertwined Destinies

Beneath the stars, our fates align,
In every heartbeat, your soul is mine.
Across the skies, our wishes soar,
In intertwined paths, we seek much more.

With whispers soft and laughter bright,
We chart our course, through day and night.
In every challenge, hand in hand,
Together we rise, together we stand.

The threads of time, a fabric true,
In every moment, it's me and you.
With every heartbeat, our dreams ignite,
In the canvas of life, we paint the light.

As seasons change and rivers flow,
In love's embrace, we come to know.
Each day unfolds a brand new dawn,
In intertwined destinies, we carry on.

Through the labyrinth of time, we weave,
With courage to love, we can believe.
In every heartbeat, a promise stays,
In the journey of us, throughout our days.

Pulse of Intimacy

In shadows where whispers reside,
Hearts gather and secrets abide.
The touch of a hand, gentle and warm,
In this quiet space, emotions form.

Eyes locked in a spellbound gaze,
Each moment lingers, a delicate blaze.
A dance of two souls, rhythm divine,
Time pauses, as destinies entwine.

The heartbeat echoes, soft and true,
A symphony played just for two.
Trust builds in the silence shared,
In this sacred bond, we are bared.

Words unspoken, but deeply felt,
In the warmth of the love we melt.
With every breath, a promise made,
In this pulse, our fears do fade.

Together we navigate the night,
In the dark, we find our light.
A journey, a tale, just begun,
In the pulse of intimacy, we are one.

Balance in the Boogie

Beneath the neon's vibrant glow,
Two bodies move, neither too slow.
A rhythm found, electric embrace,
In every twist, we find our place.

Feet shuffle to the beat of the night,
Spinning, twirling, a dazzling sight.
Laughter bubbles, joy takes flight,
In harmony's dance, everything's right.

Side by side, we lose all track,
In this dance that pulls us back.
The world outside fades away,
In our balance, we choose to stay.

Hearts racing fast, and spirits free,
In this moment, just you and me.
Every sway, a story to tell,
In the rhythm of life, we dwell.

The final note rings out with grace,
In the echoes, we still find our space.
With a smile, we know this groove,
In the balance, our hearts improve.

Duets in Time

Two voices blend, a perfect match,
In harmony's song, no need to attach.
Each note a step in our shared dance,
Together we weave, lost in the trance.

Time ticks gently, like a soft breeze,
Every measure a moment to seize.
With every verse, our spirits align,
In the melody's arc, we intertwine.

The chorus lifts, we rise anew,
Echoing hearts beat steady and true.
In the silence, our whispers confide,
In this duet, love cannot hide.

As the music swells, we find our way,
Each lyric a promise we softly say.
In the rhythm of life, we play our role,
With each note, we touch the soul.

The final chord fades into the night,
Yet the memory glimmers, a beautiful sight.
For in every duet, a journey we chart,
In the music of time, we are never apart.

Crescendo of Companionship

In the gentle dusk, we start to soar,
Two lives entwined, forevermore.
As laughter rings, a sweet refrain,
In this crescendo, love is our gain.

Step by step, we build our song,
In every heartbeat, we belong.
With gentle whispers, we map the stars,
In this symphony, we heal the scars.

The challenges faced, a rhythm of trust,
In the face of storms, we adapt and adjust.
With unity strong, we rise above,
In this crescendo, we find our love.

As the climax builds, we stand hand in hand,
Facing the world, united we stand.
With every high and every low,
In this duet, our feelings flow.

And as the last notes softly play,
We cherish the journey, come what may.
For in this crescendo, the truth remains,
In companionship's embrace, love sustains.

Celebrating Us

In every laugh, a spark ignites,
Together we dance through day and night.
Hand in hand, we face the tide,
With you by my side, I take pride.

Dreams woven deep in the stars above,
In our shared journey, we find love.
Through storms and calm, we stay so strong,
In the melody of life, we belong.

Memories painted with vibrant hues,
In this canvas, all we choose.
From whispers soft to shouts so loud,
Together we rise, forever proud.

Every moment, a treasure to hold,
In the stories of us, forever told.
With hearts aglow, we light the way,
In the celebration, we find our sway.

Side by side, as time will tell,
In the echoes of joy, we dwell.
With every heartbeat, we embrace the us,
In this beautiful journey, it's just us.

Weaving Together

Threads of laughter, bright and bold,
In the fabric of life, stories unfold.
Each moment stitched with care and grace,
In our tapestry, we find our place.

Colors merging, a vibrant blend,
Every knot and loop, love we send.
Through the highs and lows, we create,
In the weaving, we celebrate fate.

Silken dreams float on the breeze,
In the quiet, we find our ease.
With every touch, the world feels right,
Together, we weave our shared light.

Patterns form, unique and true,
In this dance, I find you.
Hand in hand, we craft our way,
In the loom of time, forever stay.

Every thread tells a tale anew,
In the bond, we are two.
Bound together, a story immense,
Weaving our hearts, our love, our sense.

Silhouettes in the Sunset

Against the sky, we stand so tall,
Silhouettes dancing, answering the call.
With colors blazing, the day meets night,
In the fading glow, everything feels right.

Whispers of wind through the trees,
Carrying secrets, comforting pleas.
In the golden hour, our shadows blend,
Together forever, as time will suspend.

Moments captured in a warm embrace,
Every heartbeat a gentle trace.
The world slows down, our worries fade,
In the sunset's glow, our dreams cascade.

Outlined by hues of orange and red,
In the stillness, all that needs said.
With palms entwined, we face the light,
Silhouettes merging, hearts taking flight.

As the sun dips low, the night awakes,
In this twilight, true love never breaks.
With every sunset, a promise made,
In the beauty of dusk, memories cascade.

Embracing Echoes

In the quiet, echoes softly sound,
Whispers of love in the air surround.
Each heartbeat echoes through the night,
In the silence, we feel the light.

Memories linger like a sweet refrain,
In the gentle breeze, the love remains.
Through mountains high and valleys low,
In the echoes, our spirit will grow.

Every laugh, a melody sweet,
In this symphony, our hearts meet.
With every word, we weave a song,
In the embrace where we belong.

Time may pass, yet we hold tight,
In the embrace of love, all feels right.
Through shadows cast, we shine so bright,
In the echoes of dawn, we take flight.

With you near, our voices entwined,
In the library of moments, memories bind.
Embracing echoes, we journey forth,
Together we dance, revealing worth.

Gusset of Grace

In the seam of silence, we find,
A gentle fold that holds the kind.
Whispers envelop, life's embrace,
In every stitch, a thread of grace.

Torn edges mend with tender care,
Worn paths reveal a beauty rare.
Lost moments woven tight like lace,
In the fabric of love, we trace.

Every tear a story told,
In vibrant hues from deep and bold.
Uplifting tales in every space,
Worn fabric sings of time and place.

As daylight dawns, the shadows fade,
In every fold, a promise laid.
With every heartbeat, we embrace,
The tender touch of Gusset's grace.

Notes from the Heartstrings

In quiet corners, melodies hum,
Soft echoes play where dreams succumb.
Strings pulled taut with love's refrain,
In every note, a joy or pain.

Dancing shadows in twilight's glow,
Whispers of secrets only we know.
Harmonics weave through time and space,
The sweet serenade of heartstrings' grace.

Each heartbeat a gentle stroke,
From sorrow's depths, new hopes awoke.
In symphonies of smiles we chase,
The timeless tune of our embrace.

Under starlit skies, we sing,
The laughter and tears love can bring.
With every chord, we find our place,
In the music of heartstrings' grace.

Measures of Meaning

In shadows deep, we seek the light,
With every step, the heart takes flight.
Caught in the rhythm of life's embrace,
We find our worth in each small trace.

Moments captured, fleeting yet bold,
The weight of whispers, stories told.
Each breath a line in time's endless race,
Crafting our tale with measures of grace.

Through trials faced, we rise and bend,
In every struggle, we make amends.
Footprints linger, time can't erase,
As we map our journey, this is our place.

In laughter's echoes, dreams take flight,
In shared tomorrows, love ignites.
Each measure a testament to face,
The beauty of life in time's embrace.

Ballet of Bonds

On the stage of life, we twirl and leap,
With every heartbeat, our secrets keep.
In pirouettes of joy, we find,
The dance of souls forever intertwined.

Through whispered steps, we navigate,
In every glance, sweet love's fate.
The music swells, we find our pace,
In each other's arms, our sacred space.

As shadows play beneath the moon,
In harmony, our hearts attune.
With every lift, a soft embrace,
In this ballet, we find our grace.

In timeless rhythms, we unite,
Through soaring heights, we take flight.
Together we shine, our spirits blaze,
In the ballet of bonds, love's gentle gaze.

Language of Love

In shadows soft, our whispers glide,
Words unspoken, hearts confide.
With every glance, a tale unfolds,
In silken threads, true love extols.

Through tender touch, our souls will weave,
A tapestry of dreams believe.
In every laugh, the world ignites,
The language of love, pure delight.

Moments shared, forever stay,
In silent bonds, we drift and play.
No need for words, our hearts will know,
The beauty in this gentle flow.

Through storms and sun, we journey forth,
In every heartbeat, find our worth.
Together, dear, we paint the sky,
In love's embrace, together fly.

Whispers Beneath the Stars

Beneath the stars, we softly sway,
In quiet dreams, where shadows play.
Each twinkle holds a secret's grace,
In this vast night, we find our place.

The silver moon, a watchful eye,
Reflects our hopes as we reply.
With gentle murmurs, hearts align,
The universe, our love's design.

The constellations tell our tale,
In cosmic winds, our love won't pale.
With every sigh, the heavens dance,
In this sweet night, we find our chance.

Stars above, a map so bright,
Guiding us through the velvet night.
In whispered dreams, our spirits soar,
Together, love, forevermore.

Consonance of Caring

In tender moments, hearts align,
A symphony of love, divine.
Each note we share, a song so sweet,
In every heartbeat, we repeat.

With gentle words, we lift each other,
A melody, like no other.
Through laughter shared, our troubles fade,
In caring arms, we aren't afraid.

A harmony of souls entwined,
In every gesture, love defined.
Through storms we navigate, we stand,
In this duet, hand in hand.

Each day unfolds, a brand new tune,
In the warmth of the afternoon.
Together we rise, as one we'll glow,
In consonance, our love will flow.

Harmony in Dissonance

In chaos found, our hearts embrace,
A dance of storms, a sacred space.
For in the clash, we learn to grow,
In dissonance, our love will show.

With every clash, we find our tune,
In the dark, we dance by moon.
Through trials faced, we hold on tight,
In every struggle, love shines bright.

When tempests rage and voices rise,
We navigate beneath the skies.
In held breaths, our truths emerge,
From discord, harmony will surge.

Together we mend, piece by piece,
In each disagreement, find release.
With open hearts, we shall prevail,
In harmony, love tells its tale.

Melodies of Mutuality

In harmony we find our way,
Two voices blend, come what may.
Each note a step, a gentle sway,
Together strong, come what may.

Shared laughter dances 'neath the stars,
No distance felt, no lingering scars.
In every glance, a world is ours,
Hearts in tune, like cosmic cars.

Like rivers flow, so time unites,
Through ebb and flow, we scale new heights.
In whispered words, our future ignites,
With every breath, our love invites.

Support like sun, both warm and bright,
In shadows' grasp, we share the light.
Through storms we sail, our bond takes flight,
Together whole, in endless night.

In silent grace, we hear each call,
Two souls entwined, we rise, we fall.
In every heartbeat, we stand tall,
In melodies of mutual thrall.

Unspoken Synchrony

In quiet glances, worlds collide,
Unseen threads, through time they glide.
Where thoughts converge and hearts abide,
In unspoken synchrony, we confide.

A gentle touch, no need for words,
In this silence, magic stirs.
Like whispered winds, like nesting birds,
Our bond, a song, the heart prefers.

Through every pause, connection grows,
In shared silence, true love shows.
The heart's deep rhythm softly flows,
Where unfinalized beauty glows.

In every heartbeat, echoes reel,
An understanding, deeply real.
In quietude, we carve, we heal,
Our souls, in synchrony, congeal.

Together, we write uncharted skies,
In every glance, the universe ties.
Our hearts converse in lullabies,
In unspoken words, love never lies.

A Serenade of Souls

In twilight's grace, our voices soar,
A serenade, a sweet encore.
In rhythms soft, we explore,
Two souls entwined, forevermore.

Each note a promise, pure and bright,
In harmony, we share our light.
With every breath, we find our flight,
In serenades, our hearts ignite.

Through whispers sweet, the night unfolds,
In secrets shared, the dream beholds.
Together we stand, brave and bold,
In melodies our love enfolds.

As stars align, we dance on air,
In twirling joy, without a care.
A serenade, a vibrant prayer,
In every heartbeat, love laid bare.

Through time and space, we wander free,
In symphony, just you and me.
Our souls entwined, eternally,
In serenade, we choose to be.

Pulse of Partnership

In tandem steps, we walk the path,
Through ups and downs, through joy and wrath.
In every moment, shared our math,
Together we find our aftermath.

A pulse that beats, both strong and sure,
In partnership, our hearts endure.
With every challenge, we secure,
The bonds of love that we maintain pure.

With laughter shared, we paint the day,
In harmony, we find our way.
From dawn till dusk, come what may,
In rhythm's flow, we choose to stay.

Through trials fierce, our spirits rise,
In every glance, love's sweet surprise.
United as one, we touch the skies,
In pulse of partnership, truth lies.

The world may shift, yet here we stand,
In hands entwined, we make our stand.
A force of nature, love so grand,
With every beat, our journeys planned.

Finesse of Fragility

In whispers soft, the petals sway,
Gently kissed by morning ray.
Each moment holds a tender thread,
Life's beauty blooms where fears have fled.

Like glass that glints in sunlight's dance,
We navigate our fragile chance.
With every touch, we shape and mold,
A story woven, brave and bold.

Yet in the light, shadows creep near,
Fragility whispers, no need for fear.
Embrace the balance of strength and grace,
In vulnerability, find your place.

These fibers tremble, a soft refrain,
Through joy and sorrow, love remains.
Each tear that falls and smile that gleams,
We find our way through broken dreams.

So let us dance with hearts laid bare,
In the elegance of a gentle care.
Life's fineness blooms, a tender art,
In the rhythm of a fragile heart.

Frequencies of Friendship

In laughter shared, a bond takes flight,
With every joke, the world feels bright.
A melody in each embrace,
The harmony of a kindred space.

Through trials faced and secrets kept,
In silent moments, no tears left.
We resonate in joy and pain,
Friendship's song, our sweet refrain.

Like radio waves, we intertwine,
In frequencies where souls align.
A sanctuary built on trust,
In beautiful chaos, we find the just.

With every memory, we turn the dial,
Echoes of laughter stretching a mile.
Each voice a note in vibrant tune,
A symphony of hearts beneath the moon.

In this vast world, we hold the key,
To navigate life's vast sea.
In friendship's embrace, we find our way,
A guiding light, come what may.

Threads of Trust

Woven closely, our hearts entwine,
With whispers soft, the stars align.
In quiet moments, we lay bare,
A tapestry of dreams to share.

Each thread a promise, strong yet fine,
In trust we cultivate, a sacred vine.
Through storms we stand, the fabric tight,
In the darkest hours, we find our light.

The stitches formed in laughter's glow,
In shared adventures, watch us grow.
Through trials faced, our bond remains,
In joyful hearts, no room for chains.

In every knot, a tale is spun,
A journey shared, united as one.
Through time we stitch, with care and grace,
In trust's embrace, we find our place.

The threads may fray, but we won't part,
In every woven moment, we find art.
Together strong, through thick and thin,
A masterpiece crafted, where love begins.

The Pulse of Connection

In hurried beats, our hearts collide,
With every glance, we cannot hide.
A rhythm found in silent stares,
A dance of souls, free from cares.

Through distances that stretch and bend,
Each heartbeat tells where journeys end.
In whispered dreams, we share our fears,
The pulse of life, through countless years.

Like waves that crash on shores unseen,
In every touch, a world between.
The energy flows, electric touch,
In connection's grasp, we find so much.

In laughter's echo, in tears' release,
Each bond we forge, a special peace.
Within this pulse, we come alive,
Through every joy, we learn to thrive.

Together we grow, entwined and bold,
In the warmth of hearts, a story told.
The pulse of life, our guiding song,
In every beat, we all belong.

Threads of Affinity

In twilight's glow, we weave our dreams,
Soft whispers linger, or so it seems.
With every thread, our souls entwine,
In quiet moments, your heart meets mine.

Beneath the stars, our stories blend,
Invisible bonds that never end.
Though miles apart, our spirits soar,
In every heartbeat, I long for more.

The tapestry of us, so rich and bright,
Colors of laughter, gleams of light.
Together we conquer, together we rise,
A journey crafted beneath vast skies.

Each thread a promise, a silent vow,
In this shared space, I cherish how.
The warmth of you, my guiding star,
No distance matters, no dream too far.

Embroidered moments in silver and gold,
Our tale of yearning, beautifully told.
With every stitch, the love expands,
In the fabric of time, we hold hands.

Cadence of Closeness

With every heartbeat, a rhythm flows,
In the dance of trust, our love bestows.
A gentle pulse beneath the skin,
Sings of the bond that draws us in.

In quiet corners, we share a glance,
An unspoken language, a sacred dance.
Your laughter echoes, a sweet refrain,
In crowded rooms, we feel the same.

Through whispered secrets and soft embrace,
We treasure this delicate, shared space.
Each touch a note in this melody,
Composed together, just you and me.

In twilight's hush, we find our way,
A song of closeness that words can't say.
As shadows blend, we draw near,
In the cadence of love, I hold you dear.

With every moment, our hearts align,
A symphony of souls, beautifully entwined.
In unity, we rise above,
The blessed cadence of endless love.

Whispers in Unison

In the cool of night, whispers collide,
Two hearts in rhythm, our secrets reside.
With gentle tones, your voice finds me,
A serenade soft, eternally free.

Through soft caress and lingering gaze,
We dance in silence, enrapt in a haze.
Your laughter twinkles like stars above,
A melody woven through acts of love.

In sacred spaces, our spirits blend,
Shared breaths of promise, love's sweet mend.
With every sigh, we trace the night,
In whispers shared, we ignite delight.

The world fades away as we silently speak,
In timeless moments, it's connection we seek.
As shadows stretch, our stories bloom,
In cherished whispers, there's no room for gloom.

Through every conflict, laughter, and tears,
Our whispers unite, dispelling all fears.
In harmony crafted, we find our way,
In whispers of love, forever we stay.

Notes of Love's Journey

In the dawn's light, melodies rise,
With every step, hope fills the skies.
A symphony starts on this winding road,
In the dance of life, we share the load.

Every laughter brightens the day,
Each shared moment, a gentle sway.
Soft notes carry whispers of fate,
In this journey together, we resonate.

Through trials faced and joys embraced,
For each fleeting moment, our hearts are graced.
In chorus we sing, for troubles shall pass,
In love's sweet refrain, we find peace at last.

As seasons change, our tune evolves,
In harmony crafted, our love resolves.
Forever entwined, we can't go wrong,
In the notes of love, we find our song.

With endless chapters and verses to come,
The music of us is far from done.
In this journey together, forever we'll stay,
In the notes of love, we find our way.